Perspectives
Living With the Weather
What Are the Challenges?

Series Consultant: Linda Hoyt

Flying Start
to Literacy

Contents

How much should we rely on modern technology to protect us from extremes of climate?

People have been able to live in extreme climates for thousands of years. They have done so by building appropriate housing and wearing the right clothing when they venture outdoors. Today, modern technology makes it easy for people to live comfortably in all sorts of climates.

But are we wasting precious resources to keep ourselves comfortable? What are the alternatives?

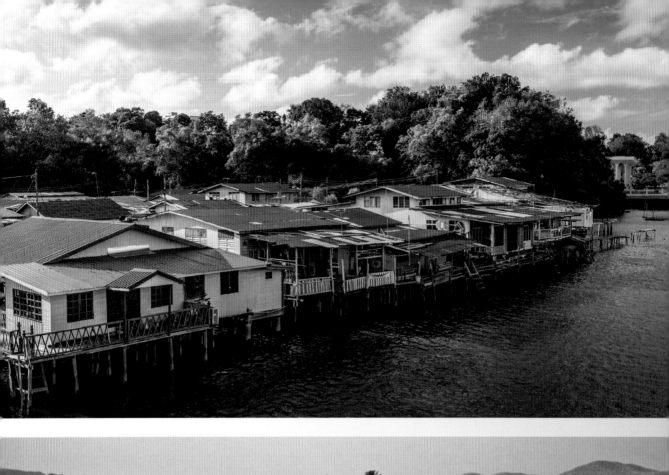

Homes that master the weather

From hot, dry deserts to windy, freezing steppes, the earth has extreme climates. People who live in these harsh climates must adapt to them.

In this article, journalist Margaret Macalister Slepkow tells us about people who have built homes that protect them from extreme heat and extreme cold without using modern technology.

What can we learn from these people about building environmentally appropriate homes?

Deep in the earth

The village of Matmata, Tunisia, lies on the edge of the Sahara Desert. On a summer day, the sun bakes the land to 43 degrees Celsius or more. But nighttime temperatures may be as low as four degrees Celsius. Moisture in the air holds heat. Temperatures in Matmata drop because the dry desert air cannot hold heat.

To escape the burning sun and the nighttime chill, people in Matmata live in underground caves. Villagers dig large holes six metres into the ground. Ramps or staircases lead down to these holes. The holes serve as courtyards for attached underground rooms. Tunnels connect the rooms. People even carve their furniture from the rock walls.

The caves stay a constant temperature. The thick sandstone walls absorb the sun's heat and stay warm throughout the night. By morning they have cooled off. They remain cool during the day while they slowly absorb heat from the sun. At dusk, the cycle begins again.

This door leads to an underground house in Matmata, Tunisia.

A water village

In the Southeast Asian country of Brunei, people must adapt to a tropical climate. Located along the equator, Brunei is hot and humid. Temperatures range from 24 degrees Celsius to 33 degrees Celsius. It rains often, and the air is hot and sticky.

The South China Sea borders Brunei on the north. Strong ocean winds fan Brunei's coast. These winds travel up the Brunei River.

The cool air they deliver brings some relief from the tropical climate. The village of Kampong Ayer makes good use of these breezes. The homes in this "water village" stand on stilts above the water. The sea breezes act as fans, circulating air through open windows.

Many families in Kampong Ayer also use ceiling fans to keep cool. The river plays a vital role in helping villagers adapt to the heat. People swim in the cool shade beneath the houses. Children in Kampong Ayer learn to swim before they learn to walk.

The water village of Kampong Ayer in Brunei, Southeast Asia

Circular homes

More than 8000 kilometres north of Brunei are the steppe lands of central Asia. The steppes are large, dry grasslands. These grasslands are home to nomads who move from place to place with their herds of sheep and goats.

In the summer, nomads graze their herds in cool mountain pastures. In the winter, they move them to warmer valleys. Because they migrate often, nomads need homes that are easy to move. These homes must also protect them from winter temperatures of −45 degrees Celsius.

Assembling a traditional Mongolian house – called a *ger* – in Mongolia.

Nomads in the steppes live in circular tents called *gers* (or yurts). Gers are wooden frames covered with felt. Their shape helps to deflect the steppes' icy winds. The felt covering repels snow and rain. It also holds in the heat given off by stoves inside the *ger*. A hole in the roof lets light in and lets smoke escape.

These amazing dwellings are examples of how people master the weather. Whether it's hot or cold outside, these homes are comfortable shelters from harsh climates.

The layers of felt on a *ger* are covered in waterproof canvas and secured with straps.

Gardens in the sky

Cities are hot places. Tall office buildings, apartment buildings, pavements and roadways trap heat so that a city is always many degrees warmer than the surrounding suburbs. In this article, journalist Marcia Amidon Lusted describes one way of cooling cities in summer and keeping them warmer in winter.

What do you think about this solution to making a city more liveable? Do you have any other ideas?

Do sky gardens seem like a fantasy?

Not at all. Many skyscrapers and other tall city buildings are now "going green". Green roofs are becoming more common in large cities, as a contrast to the hot cement of streets and buildings. And these green roofs aren't just for show. They actually serve several important purposes.

A city can be a very hot place. On a summer day, the roof of a building can reach almost 93 degrees Celsius. That's almost hot enough to cook an egg! And as the global climate heats up, cities are only getting hotter.

But by installing green roofs, which are covered with living matter like grass, leafy plants, and even vegetables and herbs, buildings do not heat up as much. They stay cooler in the summer and warmer in the winter, especially as the roof garden grows and thickens.

Green roofs absorb more rainwater, too. So the water doesn't have to be drained away or wash through city streets. A green roof is also a place to grow food, like fresh vegetables. Instead of relying on farmers in far-off places and food that has to be trucked into the city, city dwellers can grow some of their own.

These gardens in the sky do require careful planning. The roof has to be relatively flat and strong enough to support the weight of soil, plants and water. The roof must be covered with a tough, waterproof barrier to keep water from leaking down inside. And the soil must be covered, at least until the plants grow, to keep it from blowing away, since roofs are very windy places.

So remember – a skyscraper doesn't have to have a hot, boring asphalt roof. It can be a wonderful garden in the sky – and maybe a spot for your next picnic.

Too hot, too cold

Even in mild climates, we can have periods of very hot or very cold weather. Our reaction is usually to turn on the air-conditioning or heating.

What other ways are there to maintain a comfortable temperature?

"I hate the hot weather. I don't like being hot at all. When it's hot outside, I turn up the air-conditioning in our house. And when it's cold, I turn up the heating. It's easy. Why should I do anything different?"

"I don't like being hot either, but using air-conditioning all the time is not good for the environment. There are lots of other ways to stay cool.

The best thing about our house is the trees. There is a big tree at the front of our house that faces north and keeps our house cool all summer. There are two more trees on the west side of the house where the afternoon sun could make it very hot.

Even when it's really hot, I like to sit under the tree in the front because it's cool and breezy. In autumn, the trees lose their leaves and the sun can warm our house as the weather becomes cooler. I don't mind raking up the leaves in autumn!"

"It used to be really cold in our house. Dad said it was because our house was 'leaking heat'. So we fixed our house. We put insulation in the roof and in the walls. We sealed up all the places where cold air could get in. And we replaced all the windows with double glazing. Now our house stays really warm without turning up the heating. And not only is our house warmer in winter – it is cooler in summer!"

"Putting shutters on windows has an amazing effect. They keep a house cool by keeping the sun off the windows, and they let the breeze blow through when the slats are open. When you close the shutters and close the slats, the shutters keep the cold out and the heat in. And they provide security and protection from storms in winter. Also, I think they look amazing!"

"I live on the 16th floor in an apartment building and our apartment never gets cold. We don't often have to turn on the heating because the heat from all the other apartments rises up and keeps our place warm. But the apartment is hot in summer. Dad put in ceiling fans and they really make a difference. They keep the air moving and I sleep well, even on very hot nights.

I like to feel cosy in winter. I wear hats, and warm socks, and jumpers. And I love having a cup of hot chocolate. It warms me up. Mum puts warm flannelette sheets on our beds and extra blankets. We don't turn the heating up high and it saves us a lot of money."

The coolest thing to do in Dubai

Fun-seekers in the United Arab Emirates (UAE) often hit the slopes of Ski Dubai for hours of downhill skiing, snowboarding, sledding or tobogganing.

What's so unusual about that? asks journalist Sylvia Whitman. This Ski Dubai mountain is in the middle of a shopping mall on the edge of a desert!

Is this just good fun? What ethical issues, such as the waste of precious resources, need to be considered?

Ski run in the sun

Dubai is one of the seven states that make up the UAE. In August, the daily high temperature averages 41 degrees Celsius. Even in winter, the thermometre never falls below 15 degrees Celsius.

Before Ski Dubai opened in 2005, many people who live in Dubai, the Emiratis, had never seen snow. Traditional pastimes reflected life in the desert. People raced camels, raised falcons and gathered for poetry contests. Along the coast, fishers and pearl divers swam and competed in boat building. Social life centered around the family.

The city of Dubai is in the Arabian Desert, on the edge of the Persian Gulf.

After the discovery of oil in the 1960s, Dubai became very wealthy. Ruling families began to think big – really big. They decided to turn the capital city of Dubai into a luxurious tourist destination and created an enormous indoor ski resort in the Mall of the Emirates. Twenty-five storeys high, Ski Dubai can hold 1500 guests.

Every morning, it "snows" 60 centimetres in Dubai! Snow guns spray water into freezing air that has been "seeded" with tiny particles – ice, clay, even soap flakes – and snow falls to the ground. Any melted water runs off through the air-conditioning tubes and waters gardens around the mall.

This restaurant at the Mall of the Emirates has a view over the ski slopes of Ski Dubai.

The indoor ski resort, Ski Dubai, covers just over 22,500 square metres. It has five ski slopes.

When Emiratis come to Ski Dubai, they rent everything: skis or snowboards, poles, jackets, pants, boots and even disposable socks, since traditional Emirati clothing – a long white shirtdress (*kandura*) for men and a black robe-like dress (*abaya*) for women – doesn't suit the slopes. Skiing is new to Dubai, but Emiratis still enjoy it as a family, whether playing in the snow or watching from the mall.

What is your opinion?: How to write a persuasive argument

1. State your opinion

Think about the issues related to your topic. What is your opinion?

2. Research

Research the information you need to support your opinion.

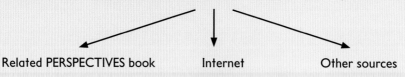

Related PERSPECTIVES book   Internet   Other sources

3. Make a plan

Introduction

How will you "hook" the reader?

State your opinion.

List reasons to support your opinion.

What persuasive devices will you use?

Reason 1	**Reason 2**	**Reason 3**
Support your reason with evidence and details.	Support your reason with evidence and details.	Support your reason with evidence and details.

Conclusion

Restate your opinion. Leave your reader with a strong message.

4. Publish

Publish your persuasive argument.

Use visuals to reinforce your opinion.